Theme behind building ALEAP, India

People, Purpose, Principles

Charith Venkat Pidikiti

February 2019

Author

Charith is a 1986 born, globetrotter and a biomedical engineer, who currently lives in Munich, Germany. A true jack-of-all-trades who religiously follows four words, "Ambition has no limits". Apart from being a full time employee at a Fortune 500 company, he is also an entrepreneur, an artist, a drummer, a fitness aficionado and a writer, who loves and collects classic cars and history books.

Hailing from India, a country rich in diverse religions and varied cultures, he was always obsessed with history, mythology and religion, yet it was his penchant for science since a young age that led him to study at the New York University, in one of the largest cosmopolitan cities of the world, NYC. After which he moved to work in Germany, where he is currently working on his Doctorate, has accomplished over four medical and two business publications and won the "Making A Difference" Award.

He constantly travels around the world with curiosity, learning foreign traditions, cultures, religions, modern technology or simply in pursuit of new experiences.

Follow the Author:

 https://instagram.com/charithvenkat

 https://www.facebook.com/charith.venkat

Copyright © Charith Venkat Pidikiti 2018

All rights reserved

Charith Venkat Pidikiti asserts the moral right to be identified as the author of this work.

Although the author and publisher have made every effort to ensure that the information in this book was correct at press time, the author and publisher do not assume and hereby disclaim any liability to any party for any loss, damage, or disruption caused by errors or omissions, whether such errors or omissions result from negligence, accident, or any other cause.

ISBN: 9781090844828

Cover concept and Design by Alpha-X

ANNOTATION

Women are good managers. When a woman can manage a house well she can manage the business as well. Women entrepreneurship is gaining importance in India because of the policies, schemes and the incentives by the government. Organizations like ALEAP India (The Association of Lady Entrepreneurs of Andhra Pradesh) India recognizes the need to encourage women entrepreneurship and started guiding women since 1993. The programs developed by ALEAP, the hand holding support, the institutional entrepreneur development trainings and skill EDP's have widened the scope for better future. The women who owned registered firms are only 30% but there are many more women who run their businesses in an unorganized way. This has to be addressed by the government. Voluntary organizations like Aleap have come forward to help these women to sustain their businesses by availing the possible incentives and grants. Women are leaving the jobs and start their lives as entrepreneurs to have flexibility to take care of home and business. Women owned businesses are gaining importance and traction.

This book discusses how the voluntary organization ALEAP India started its journey, how its branches are emerged one after the other. It started with FAB cell (Facilitator business cell). Then it recognised the need for a piece of land to start their business, then proper training to run the business, then access to finance, then marketing etc. As these problems have raised, ALEAP has found solutions. The book covers how ALEAP is helping women entrepreneurs through their journey from 1993 until date.

KEY WORDS

Andhra
Association
Business
Corporation
Entrepreneurs
Enterprise
Government
Industry
Marketing
Organization
Pradesh
Sustainability
Telangana
Trademark
Women

TABLE OF CONTENTS

1. INTRODUCTION..9
2. ALEAP, INDIA..10
   - 2.1 TRADEMARK OF ALEAP..........................6
   - 2.2 FAB CELL..7
   - 2.3 CED...8
   - 2.4 ACGA..10
   - 2.5 A-GRIP..11
   - 2.6 NAIPUNYAM..13
   - 2.7 VANDEMATARAM...................................13
3. WECONNECT INTERNATIONAL:.........................29
4. CONCLUSIONS...33
5. BIBLIOGRAPHY AND WEB RESOURCES..............35
6. TABLE OF FIGURES..36
7. ABBREVIATIONS..37

INTRODUCTION

Research question: Brand building- Building an excellent organization for the economic empowerment of women

In India, women have limited themselves to micro and small enterprises due to traditional, socio-cultural environment. Entrepreneurship is a noble profession as they provide livelihood income to many. Many people depend directly or indirectly on entrepreneur. Entrepreneur is a national asset as every nation financial growth depends on the income generated by small-scale industry. In India "Make in India" is the slogan now and to encourage women entrepreneurship government is offering incentives and schemes for the betterment of the small-scale industry. The nation's economic growth depends on their creation of wealth. Wealth creation helps enhancing their living standards. Women in Telugu states are highly motivated to take up entrepreneurship as their preferred carrier. One of the reasons is the presence of Aleap and their services to women.

ALEAP – ASSOCIATION OF LADY ENTREPRENEURS OF ANDHRA PRADESH, INDIA

Aleap - the word that every aspiring women is looking for was founded with an aim to empower women through enterprise creation. May be a tiny business like selling milk and vegetables to the next-door neighbor or a grocery shop, tailoring unit, a small-scale industry etc.

The idea of starting this organization has come to Mrs. Rama Devi who is an entrepreneur herself. Being an entrepreneur, she knows how difficult it is to get all the necessary permissions to start a business.

She has the sympathy for other women in business who are struggling to sustain in their business. The idea to help other women came into her mind and she gave a lot of thought to implement her idea. In her struggling, few other women joined her and assured to extend a helping hand[1].

The initial decision was to join in FAPCCI, The Federation of Andhra Pradesh Chamber of Commerce and Industry, a male dominated organization for business people.

They tried to disseminate information to the people from FAPCCI but it did not help much. Later they decided to start a women's wing, which did not work. They all collectively decide

---

[1] Women in Higher Education in India: Perspectives and Challenges Front Cover Hari Ponnamma Rani, Madhavi Kesari Cambridge Scholars Publishing, 27 Jul 2018

to start an organization exclusively for and named it ALEAP on December 18 1993, registered under section 25 of companies act.

The name given to the organization has two meanings. "A-leap", a big jump from a normal woman to an entrepreneur. The other idea was Association Lady Entrepreneurs of Andhra Pradesh. It was started as an organization confined to the state. Now it is a national body with ALEAP as a trademark. After Aleap became a national body, the name changed to ALEAP India.

2.1 Trademarks of aleap

Now Aleap is an organization where members feel proud of the name, which is known to all the government organizations as well as NGO's (Non governmental organizations). The founder member Mrs Rama Devi is a visionary who strives to bring economic empowerment to the women through enterprise creation. To achieve this she and her colleague Dr Jyothi Rao Pidikiti liased with the Government, both state and nation and with the financial support they have implemented many projects[2].

Now Aleap is a brand many organizations are looking for guidance.

Figure 1, ALEAP Logo (Source: www.aleap.org)

Since 1993 Aleap has developed thousands of entrepreneurs and now it is the most sort after platform to get information

---

[2] State-Business Relations and Economic Development in Africa and India Front Cover Kunal Sen Routledge, 7 May 2013

regarding business. The platform helps gain knowledge as well as facilitates the conversion of their idea into a business. Any one with an aim to become an entrepreneur can become a member of Aleap. Girls with minimum education, women of any age, married or seperated, women without proper jobs are all eligible to be the members and avail services from Aleap. Women with pull or push come to aleap for support. Aleap believes that they are self motivated, they come with a determination to be independent. The common quality in them is the determination to face challenges, They are prepared to face risks. With a little helping hand they are ready to work hard and establish themselves as able entrepreneurs.

The first step was to identify women who are working in an unorganised way. The purpose of this was to organise the existing businesses. Help them to register the units, guide them to access finance, help them to utilise the incentives offered by the government. Aleap is the home for women who want to support other women in establishing the business. It is one of the largest women entrepreneur associations in India.

The main purpose is to help women economically independent. To achieve its objectives aleap developed few flagship programs.

2.2 FAB cell

Facilitator business cell. Aleap helps to convert the idea into business. The women who come to aleap can get all the necessary information regarding enterprise creation. Aleap has counselors to do preliminary counseling. If they come with an idea the team scrutinizes their idea. For a viable project aleap helps them in getting all the required certifications. Here members can avail the services as one stop service.

Women in today's world are playing many roles, as mother and entrepreneur. They are very important as home makers in the house and as an entrepreneur. To balance the two roles they need lot of support. They are the integral part of business, but their potentialities are not utilized to the fullest. Because lack of support from the house environment most of them are limited to small scale industry. Given an opportunity they excel.

2.3 CED

Center for entrepreneurship Development, registered under societies act. Empowerment through training and development programs. CED is the training institute for imparting training. CED caters its services for both men and women. Dr A.P.J. Abdul Kalam inaugurated the campus and in his address to the members he said CED should be repeated in all the districts of the state. He appreciated the services rendered by aleap to the nation at large.

Figure 2, Centre for Entrepreneurship Development Logo (Source: http://www.cedaleapindia.org)

CED is an ISO certified 9001:2015 organization, which was founded in 1997 by the Association of Lady Entrepreneurs of Andhra Pradesh, India (ALEAP) to create opportunities for aspiring women entrepreneurs and develop Micro, Small & Medium Enterprises in every part of the two states of Telangana and Andhra Pradesh. The organization is registered as a provider of training and development of Micro, Small and Medium Enterprises under the Societies Act.

The German organization called „The Deutsche Gesellschaft für Internationale Zusammenarbeit GmbH" and the ministry of MSME, Government of India have jointly awarded CED with a certificate of merit and an award. These were given at the national level as a recognition for being a Responsible Indian Business Management Organization and revolutionary developments in the field of entrepreneurship by providing a pro-business atmosphere to foster the progress of Micro, Small & Medium Enterprises towards their sustainable success.

Center for entrepreneurship Development offers training programs such as:

- Digital Marketing Training Program: the Digital Marketing 3 days CED created training program has the aim to bring awareness of the various digital platforms, which can be used to promote brands through numerous systems of digital media and to reach the consumers online.
- Vermicompost Training Program: The Vermicompost 3 days training program's main aim is to offer training in entrepreneurship to the accomplices who are interested in starting their own vermicompost division and generate the awareness amongst the individuals regarding the advantages of Vermicompost. As per the

plan of the program, member are training in the theory and practically in the diverse methods of vermicompost preparation. In this program, CED is training applicants of any age group, irrespective of educational background and gender.

- Self-Entrepreneurship Development Program: CED has also founded the Self-Entrepreneurship Development Program, where interested applicants pay a certain fee to commence the 12 days EDP training session. The aim of this program is to instill entrepreneurship skills via industrial/onsite visits and classroom activities. CED is training applicants of any age group, irrespective of educational background and gender. 4 Self EDPs have been conducted in the previous financial year by CED.
- SIDBI Entrepreneurship Development: SIDBI (Small Industries Development Bank of India) sponsored Entrepreneurship Development program is a 12 days session to improve business standards amongst women (Scheduled cast, Scheduled tribes, women entrepreneurs etc.) and encourage their entrepreneurship choices as an ideal career. CED was able to organize two EDPs in the financial year 2016-2017. The first program was led with 31 members in Telangana, in which 15 participants established their units and the second program has been conducted with

28 Participants in the state of Andhra Pradesh, in which 10 members established their units.

The Centre for Entrepreneurship Development has been supporting the small-scale industries sector, which is the backbone of the Indian economy. After agriculture, the small-scale industries are the leading employment providers. CED helps these sectors by providing services like, training, mentoring, and monitoring etc. This in turn gives the entrepreneurs the necessary tools to develop critical thinking, creativity and developing the right product and the right business model.

In order to achieve all its objectives, the Centre for Entrepreneurship Development has been constantly upholding its worldwide network with organizations around the globe such as entrepreneurship development institutions in other countries, NGOs and training centers that are all aimed at the same goal.

2.4 ACGA

Aleap Credit Guarantee Association - A registered body developed with an inspiration of the Italian model "CONFIDI" which helps its members to access finance without collateral support. Aleap scrutinizes their projects, helps to prepare bankable project reports and recommends the banks for a collateral free loan. Aleap is the first organization in Andhra Pradesh state to implement this scheme and hence founded ACGA as a separate standalone body to serve this purpose. Aleap Credit Guarantee Association is registered as a company incorporated under the companies' act of section 25, 1956 for the purpose of the Mutual Credit Guarantee Scheme implementation.

The main objectives of ACGA are:
- To provide cost effective flow of credit to Micro, Small & Medium Enterprises and promote these sectors.
- To improve technical services in regards to choosing the entrepreneurs and also improve the comfort level of Banks.
- To solve any issues pertaining to credit by building a platform for entrepreneurs and the bankers.
- To provide financial access to the entrepreneurs from financial institutions or banks without the need for any collateral.

- To identify the right/viable entrepreneurs who are in need of credit.
- To provide corpus contributions and a mutual credit guarantee scheme to service industries and micro or small scale sectors.

Since its implementation, due to the purpose it serves and the government support for marketing, Aleap Credit Guarantee Association has had an increase in its the membership number (new entrepreneurs joining the organization). As more financial assistance is provided to the aspiring entrepreneurs, more members will be joining the associations, as the word spreads. ACGA is closely associated with banks in the public sector such as the Syndicate Bank, State Bank of India and the Andhra Bank. Governmental institutions such as the National Small Industries Corporation, Small Industries Development Bank of India, National Bank for Agriculture and Rural Development, Deposit Insurance Corporation have helped in facilitation Aleap's projects by providing financial assistance to aspiring entrepreneurs which made Aleap India become the nodal agency for the Indian government initiatives called „Standup India" and „Startup India" schemes.

2.5 A-GRIP

Aleap Green Industrial Park. Aleap has developed its first Industrial Park in the year 1997 exclusively for women. It is first of its kind in India where women have access to common facilities that are required for an industry. 160 industries are functioning in the first park. The third Industrial Park competed with 130 other parks world over and bagged first prize in converting waste to wealth. The final presentation was done in Munich Germany. GIZ has come forward to support site master plans for the Industrial Parks. The site master plan is given taking into consideration of environment, climate change, natural contours of land, water resources, alternative sources of energy etc. along with special needs for women. Infrastructure plays a vital role for any enterprise. Government should set priorities for women entrepreneurs or provide the land at a nominal cost.

Now Aleap has five industrial parks in two states. Women in the two telugu states wait for having a small piece of land for their business to start because at Aleap they get all the necessary information as well as moral support. They believe that if they work collectively their voice can be heard even to the government. They believe that collectively they can do wonders. They are now in a position to send recommendations to policy makers. The ministry of MSME, government of India asks for Aleap's recommendations before implementing any change in policy.

Aleap was the member in Prime Ministers task force for Government of India for several years. The brand Aleap is a success story for other organizations. InWent Germany identified Aleap as the lead organization in SAARC (South Asian Association for Regional Cooperation) and South African regions and sponsored training programs for capacity building of women entrepreneur organizations of the above said countries. All these businesswomen association heads were trained at Aleap, supported by InWent, Germany. Some of them repeated women industrial parks in their respective countries.

Aleap conducts seminars and conferences once in 2 years as part of their activity and provide professional help to all the members of Aleap. In one such recent conference they highlighted on the importance of the word „Green" for the industrial purpose. Green enterprise focusing on how to conserve the resources, how to make use of these resources in an efficient way, how to minimize waste, how to recycle and reuse water and how concentration more on renewable energy sources. Especially due to power and water crisis in India, Aleap wants implement all the possible ways and measures to conserve energy and resources. This helps in sustainable development of industrial park, both existing and new industrial parks. Since it is more difficult to implement this in older existing industrial parks, Aleap is inviting all the experts and even students constantly in their conferences to bring in new ideas to retrofit existing industries with renewable methods of energy usage.

Principles: help each other, grow together

Today there has been a phenomenal increase in the attention given to women entrepreneurship in the world over. Aleap recognized the importance of women entrepreneurship thirty years ago and fought continuously for its existence with a belief that small scale industry contributes for the economic development of the country. Members get inspiration by sharing the success stories of other women and motivated to succeed in their own business. The industrialists who are members of Aleap act as mentors to the budding entrepreneurs.

2.6 Naipunyam

The name given for skill training. Several training programs were organized under the name Naipunyam which was established in 2009 to create a skills ecosystem in India. Government of India is encouraging women entrepreneurship by introducing National Skill Development Policy in order to provide skill training. Aleap has a vision that if only the training is given to women it is of no use. They need handholding support to start something of their own and sustain. Aleap's mission is to provide training and encourage them for production units. Its main objective is to empower women workforce with the necessary tools, knowledge, skills and qualifications to themselves internationally competitive.

The Indian government introduced this policy in 2015 to provide a framework to all the skills related activities performed within the country, to bring them in alignment with the common standards and to link these skill activities to the demand centers.

2.7 Vandemataram

A program to train 40,500 women sponsored by Ministry of textiles Government of India in a period of three years in three sectors Garments, Jute and handicrafts. After successful training they were encouraged to start production by employing the co trainees. Loans were arranged by Aleap. The program was recognized by Ministry as the "Best Implementing Agency" in India. To provide livelihood employment to the women trained under Vandemataram, Aleap started Hub and Spoke models in garment sector and Banana bark product manufacturing in Handicraft sector. Here Hub is Aleap where Aleap negotiate with apparel exporters and get bulk orders. Material is cut at Hub and gets distributed to spoke units. Aleap has tied up with giant business people like Aditya Birla group for manufacturing shirts.

Likewise the other Hub and spoke is in Vijayawada where banana bark is collected and made into ropes. The spoke units weave baskets and some other products and get very good income for their livelihood. Aleap signed an MOU with IKEA to supply banana bark products in bulk. Two places were identified based on the availability of raw material. This unit can provide wage employment to 1000 women[3].

---

[3] By Investing In Women We Are Investing In Future Opportunities For Their Children: Vandana Verma Ikea foundation http://www.businessworld.in/article/By-Investing-In-Women-We-Are-Investing-In-Future-Opportunities-For-Their-Children-Vandana-Verma-Ikea-foundation/14-11-2017-131676

With the support of UNDP (United Nations Development Program), Aleap developed VLE's, village level entrepreneurs. The VLEs were given Trainers Training with the expectation that they in turn help rural women to take up businesses depending on the need and availability of raw material at their respective places.

In villages most of the women help the family by doing tiny businesses like tailoring, vending milk or milk products etc. Now with the help of state government schemes like DWAKRA rural women get finance with very low interest or no interest to start their business. Through these schemes they are able to sell their products through DWAKRA Bazaars. Aleap has thought of developing these women to next level by interfering with technological interventions. They were given EDP's to have an understanding of how to do business. Syllabus was prepared in local language; audio visual aids were developed for better understanding. Aleap employed center managers whose main duty is to mobilize women, motivate them to earn a livelihood.

Aleap got the certificate of Accreditation with Gold Grade from QCI (The Quality Council of India) and NABET (National Accreditation board for Educational training) for developing the first Indian industrial estate, which is exclusively for women. Mrs Rama Devi in her interview mentioned, in order to motivate students towards entrepreneurship Aleap entered into MOU with many colleges and universities.

Now with the guidance from Aleap more than hundred colleges are interested in opening an entrepreneurship cell in their premises. During the holidays, students visit Aleap Industrial Park to communicate with existing entrepreneurs. They gain theoretical as well as practical knowledge. Students from schools also visit the industries. They are allowed to see candle making, crayon making, food processing industries like biscuit/chocolate manufacturing etc. The college students are the brand ambassadors for Aleap to market itself. Once a year Aleap organizes „Open Days "where all the college students can participate in pitching their idea, participate in competitions related to enterprise creation. Major industrialists like Dr. Suchitra Ella of Bharat Biotech, Mrs Indira Dutt of KCP or Dr Renuka Datla of Biological Evans share their experiences and encourage students. The Consul General of the United States of America, Mrs Katherine Hadda was invited to Aleap and addressed the gathering. The consulate of USA invite Aleap to have one to one video interaction with women entrepreneurs of developing countries.

Aleap and the hard work of Mrs Rama Devi have brought recognition to the organization. The trade mark Aleap with its logo became very popular among the youth. For any information regarding some business the women of south India think about Aleap for a solution. Now Aleap is competing with other organizations not only locally but pan India

Aleap knows how to stand apart from other similar organizations, Aleap logo itself tells the value of the organization. The members like to tell others to join Aleap for betterment of their lives. For 25 years the membership fee was only 500 Rupees which is equal to 6 Euros per year. Members get all the benefits of attending periodical meetings to update schemes etc or they can avail services like medical camps.

In Aleap's view woman need not be educated to start a business, money is never a hurdle. Though accessing finance is difficult, Aleap helps them to get loans under CGTMSE scheme. What a woman require is strong determination to become an entrepreneur.

WECONNECT INTERNATIONAL:

With their slogan „Connecting Women's Enterprises with Market Opportunity Around the World" WEConnect international has been supporting Aleap and its endeavors through its network for marketing.
Weconnect International is a global network which connects women entrepreneurs and their businesses to buyers who are qualified, around the world.
WEConnect International educates, identifies, certifies and registers women's business enterprises based outside of the United States that are 51% or more owned, as well as controlled and managed by one or more women. These women and their businesses are then connected with multinational corporate buyers.

WEConnect International also connects these women with the world through live sessions and events such as Annual conferences and Forums where audiences are invited from across several institutions and organizations. An example is the „Think Big" conference conducted every year with speakers from big players such as managers and leaders from Accenture, Air Asia, InfoTech and Aleap India to name a few. The Think Big-Women in Business Forum is a unique podium for women business owners. The third annual Think Big - Women in Business Forum was held at Hyatt Regency Delhi on 9 October 2015, where over 400 participants, including investors, corporate buyers, industry mentors, media and women entrepreneurs came together. Notable speakers included Mittu Chandilya, CEO, AirAsia, India; Srikant Rao, Managing Director - Procurement, Asia Pacific, Accenture; and Padmaja Ruparel, President, Indian Angel Network. Think Big 2015 brought together delegates from 5 countries and 10 cities across the country for inspiring business skill training, experience sessions, peer learning, business meetings, and workshops. WEConnect International - Think Big Forum in India prepared and empowered women business owners to scale up and reach new market prospects. Members learned from a number of women entrepreneurs who shared their stories of success, and several participants took advantage of self-registration and certifications to make connections and do networking with corporate buyers. During the forum, corporate associate IBM declared its goal to acquire $35-60 Million from women business owners in India, while Intel, Walmart, Marriott and Accenture committed to purchasing more from women vendors.

Sponsors of Think Big include: certified women-owned business SuperSeva, Accenture, IBM, the Walmart Foundation, the Rockefeller Foundation, Intel, and certified women-owned business Welspun. The Think Big partners are: ALEAP, Bizdivas, Bristlecone, COWE, EMERG, eWIT, FKCCI, Her Entrepreneur Network, IIM Bangalore- NSRCEL, MAWE, Management Next, National Entrepreneurship Network, OCC, Pink Lemonade, Sheroes, TiE Bangalore, and TiE Chennai[4].

'ThinkBig 2017' was Asia's largest women entrepreneurship and economic empowerment summit that took place for the fifth time and was held in Gurugram, India. This was targeted to bring together the global corporations and connect them with Indian small-scale and medium businesses for collaboration and future trade through strategic partnerships. This provides a huge marketing platform for all the women and their projects to the world.

---

[4] https://weconnectinternational.org http://www.businessworld.in/article/By-Investing-In-Women-We-Are-Investing-In-Future-Opportunities-For-Their-Children-Vandana-Verma-Ikea-foundation/14-11-2017-131676/

Interactive sessions were held to discuss how women have been progressing from job seekers to job creators where pioneers who were part of the panel participated by sharing information, the challenges, their experiences, knowledge, success stories and advices regarding the field of women empowerment. The panel included bid names such as Vandana Verma, the Program Director of IKEA Foundation; Aloka Majumdar is Senior Vice President and Head of Corporate Sustainability for HSBC India; Mrs. B. kavitha Rajesh. Treasurer, ALEAP India and Conference Exhibition head. Dr Abhinav Mathur, Founding Partner, Massive Fund and Incubator moderated the program.

The treasurer of ALEAP, Mrs. Kavita Rajesh explained the significance of skilling, and quoted, "Education isn't a requirement for entrepreneurship, only zeal." She also shared the information regarding their programs such as "Vandemataram" and how they empower women through these programs. This gave the audience the sense for importance of such collaborative efforts and the need for banks to promote these efforts and provide credit and loans to the women seeking such aid. She also explained the importance for closing the information gap through mentorship, which Aleap primarily does. By mentoring these aspiring women to become successful entrepreneurs, they will understand the right industries to setup and stay motivated to reach great heights.

CONCLUSIONS

Women in southern states of India like to help the family by adding income from wage employment. These jobs either small job like a teacher or a corporate job offers security like a shell. Entrepreneurship is very different; entrepreneur is a loner with no leaves, no prescribed time, no number of working hours, and no comfortable office. She is the boss and same time a worker. The women who wants to become an entrepreneur should be ready to take challenges and sudden changes. Sometimes when you have no orders, you worry. When there are orders she may not have enough workforce to implement, she may not have enough working capital etc. These are the few challenges an entrepreneur has to face.

Always think, "We will" before starting a business, this is Aleap's motto. Aleap advises to start a business for themselves not because someone advised them to start. Before starting a business an entrepreneur should question herself Why, How, where, whom to supply, why not is also very important. She should totally convince herself before entering into a business.

Through achieving awards and accolades and global recognition from other big preexisting organizations that have already established themselves very well, Aleap has managed to reach all the end of the world. Their marketing has been mainly through the support of the media and the government education women about the existence and purpose of Aleap and all its start-ups in turn. The world now talks about Aleap since they know the achievements and the work done by its members. From the past 20 years ALEAP is striving to make, the state of Andhra Pradesh empowered through promoting women entrepreneurship. ALEAP's aim is to make the women economically independent, through motivation, counselling, training and hand holding. Accordingly, during the last two decades, increasing number of women have entered the field of entrepreneurship and they are gradually changing the face of economy of Andhra Pradesh and Telangana5.

Aleap's vision is "To become a center for excellence for development of women entrepreneurship, to foster women entrepreneurship with a focus an innovative creativity, financial sustainability and social impact.", and through this vision it has achieved great recognition.

---

[5] Asian Agribusiness Management: Case Studies in Growth, Marketing, and Upgrading Strategies Front Cover Christy Ralph D, Bernardo Joselito, Hampel-milagrosa Aimee, World Scientific, 14 Aug 2018

BIBLIOGRAPHY AND WEB RESOURCES

- Asian Agribusiness Management: Case Studies in Growth, Marketing, and Upgrading Strategies Front Cover Christy Ralph D, Bernardo Joselito, Hampel-milagrosa Aimee, World Scientific, 14 Aug 2018
- By Investing In Women We Are Investing In Future Opportunities For Their Children: Vandana Verma Ikea foundation http://www.businessworld.in/article/By-Investing-In-Women-We-Are-Investing-In-Future-Opportunities-For-Their-Children-Vandana-Verma-Ikea-foundation/14-11-2017-131676, Nina Kler, 14 November 2017
- WEConnect International in India held its second Think Big Women in Business Forum, https://weconnectinternational.org, WeConnect International.
- Women in Higher Education in India: Perspectives and Challenges Front Cover Hari Ponnamma Rani, Madhavi Kesari Cambridge Scholars Publishing, 27 Jul 2018

- State-Business Relations and Economic Development in Africa and India Front Cover Kunal Sen Routledge, 7 May 2013

TABLE OF FIGURES

Figure 1	ALEAP Logo (Source: www.aleap.org)
Figure 2	CED Logo (Source: http://www.cedaleapindia.org)

ABBREVIATIONS

ACGA	Aleap Credit Guarantee Association
ALEAP	Association Of Lady Entrepreneurs Of Andhra Pradesh
CED	Centre for Entrepreneurship Development
CONFIDI	Consorzio di garanzia collettiva dei fidi
DWCRA	DEVELOPMENT OF WOMEN AND CHILDREN IN RURAL AREAS
EDP	Entrepreneurship Development Program
FAB	Facilitator Business
FAPCCI	Federation of Andhra Pradesh Chamber of Commerce and Industry
MOU	memorandum of understanding
NABET	National Accreditation board for Educational training
NGO	Non-Governmental Organization
SAARC	South Asian Association for Regional Cooperation
SIDBI	Small Industries Development Bank of India
UNDP	United Nations Development Program
VLE	Village level entrepreneurs

www.ingramcontent.com/pod-product-compliance
Lightning Source LLC
Chambersburg PA
CBHW021852170526
45157CB00006B/2405